The Tour

BARTER to BLOCKCHAIN and BEYOND

Evolution of Trade and Money

2nd Edition

John Wnuk

ISBN: 978-0-578-61317-8

The contents of this book are intended to answer questions from newbies, wannabe experts and crypto geezers. It is not investment advice but provides education about the evolution of trade and money.

Evolution never stops -- live in the past or diversify.

John's choice to diversify with cryptocurrencies started in 2013. His wife Sherri has supported this modern innovation and contributed to this book through her review and professional editing.

Contents

Figures

Sections

Contents

A. END GAME

The purpose of this book is to provide education about the evolution of trade and money as viewed from outside the financial box. Evolution never stops. A view from outside the box may provide insight to what causes and limits change. Understanding more from the context of innovations, habits, and values, may help reveal opportunities and what is next in that evolution.

1) Innovations. Humankind tends to favor innovations that provide time savings or lifestyle benefits. A few examples are: automobile vs. horse and buggy, electric lights vs. candles, telephone vs. pony express, computer with word processing vs. typewriter, and Internet browsing vs. encyclopedia. Advances in computing, communications, and Augmented Intelligence (AI) are modern tools for pioneers of the innovations of tomorrow.

2) Habits. Money habits can challenge reason. There is a bond to the U.S. Dollar (USD) that is not backed by anything tangible. Many think the dollar is backed by gold, but it is not. The dollar went off the gold standard in 1971 and does not have intrinsic value like gold or silver. Also, the term "fiat" can be misleading. For most, it is a car, but the dollar is fiat money. That means it has value by government decree and is backed only by debt.

3) Values. The fiat dollar, as paper or deposit, does have value as a convenient means of trade. The dollar also replaced the British pound as the world reserve currency in 1944 -- as other countries are confident that the U.S. can pay its debts. The bond to fiat money, however, can hinder an understanding of what is new.

The Tour

For example, in 2009 an innovation based on mathematics and cryptography was created. It was an Electronic Cash System called "Bitcoin" with ticker symbol "BTC." That system included a "Blockchain" public ledger of peer-to-peer transactions.

Bitcoin had no established value until May, 2010. At that time, a computer programmer Laszlo Hanyecz wanted to know if he could buy anything with his Bitcoin mining rewards. He ordered two large pizzas worth about $30 and offered to pay with 10,000 Bitcoin (BTC). Laszlo enjoy his pizzas and that event is celebrated every May 22nd as Bitcoin Pizza Day. In 2010, a Bitcoin was worth $30/10,000 BTC = $0.003/BTC or about three for a penny. Today, 10,000 BTC would be worth about $10,000/BTC x 10,000 BTC = $100M. Wow, how many are in your wallet?

Bitcoin was designed to bypass existing financial institutions and prevent double spends. Bypassing financial institutions, such as banks, eliminated costs and delays of 3rd party brokers. Preventing double spends with cryptographic methods is similar to preventing spending of counterfeit fiat money. With cryptography as a base, Bitcoin is referred to as a "cryptocurrency," or "crypto." Other popular terms include "virtual currency," "Internet money," "modern money," "digital asset," and "crypto asset." Parlance of the trade also includes "coin," "Altcoin," "stablecoin," "ERC-20 token," "token," "ERC-20 coupon," or "coupon."

With the success of Bitcoin over the last decade, other crypto followed, each with their own blockchain or Distributed Ledger Technology (DLT). For current details on values, websites, whitepapers, and more, see *coinmarketcap.com/*.

Why crypto has value and other basic concepts about money, however, continues to be a mystery to many.

B. MYSTERIES

The Federal Reserve System (Fed) has existed for over a century but why it exists and what it does is a mystery to many. Very few understand how fiat money works and that is an important step to understanding crypto. Mystery also surrounds Satoshi Nakamoto the inventor of Bitcoin. Why his volatile Electronic Cash System has value and is not a scam is another mystery. This lack of understanding of basic money concepts can limit or misguide future choices in life.

1) Fed. Over a century ago, on a so called "duck hunt" on Jekyll Island, several wealthy U.S. business persons met in secret and established the foundations for a national financial system or central bank for the U.S. That system, created to prevent bank failures, now sets monetary policy, mints and prints fiat money as needed, and generates billions in profit that is sent to the U.S. Treasury every year. However, is it a mystery that a system is reporting billions in profits for a nation that is trillions in debt?

2) Satoshi. The inventor of Bitcoin and Blockchain has been a mystery for over a decade. Who is Satoshi Nakamoto? There are lots of clues about one of the richest persons on earth, but no answers. One wonders why remaining anonymous was a chosen lifestyle?

3) Electronic Cash. Another mystery is more complex. How could a volatile crypto system achieve billions in value in a few years, while aging fiat systems with so called "stable" values have spiraling debt? Sadly, the fiat debt question tends to be avoided, or worse, put down by naysayers with distorted views suggesting that insidious spiraling debt is OK, but healthy market volatility is not.

4) Choices. What is new can tend to be distrusted at first. Considering the evolution of trade and money, there is something new all the time -- from barter to brokers to banks to blockchains to what is next. But, it is a choice to participate in that evolution.

The Tour

Many choose not to participate and prefer to live in the comfort of the past. Those that choose to participate have an opportunity to diversify. They can become more informed and connect the dots between the limited tangibles of the past and the unlimited future creations of humankind. To help with better choices, suggested reading in this book and a digest of key contents are as follows:

a) Newbies can start by learning the mechanics of the dollar. If the dollar is not understood, it is unlikely that crypto will ever be understood. Start with Section C on pages 5-6 and then read Section E on pages 15-16.

b) Wannabe experts can start by reading the Epilogue. Understanding the Blockchain is a must. Read pages 46-47. Make a transaction between wallets and observe that transaction on the Blockchain. Next, read The Coiner Poem on pages 48-49. The poem can give an interesting overview of crypto technology.

c) Crypto geezers can learn more about what is beyond the blockchain. Start with Section F on page 17. After reading a few pages, take a coffee break. Continue reading, take breaks, and complete *The Tour*.

d) Of the 5,000+ existing crypto, which could likely flourish in the future? No one knows for sure, but blockchain-based crypto will likely continue including Bitcoin (BTC) as digital gold, Ethereum (ETH) as a programmable platform for Altcoins, and Cardano (ADA) with a comprehensive long term development roadmap. Beyond blockchain, an effective and efficient criteria could identify crypto and DLT that will flourish. Effective crypto would be fast, economic, and secure. Efficient crypto would use the right methods for transaction verification, ledger accounting, and cryptographic security. That criteria would filter to at least IOTA (MIOTA), Nano (NANO) and Holo (HOT) as described on pages 16-17, and c) and d) on page 31. Lots more ahead with the choice to participate in the evolution of trade and money.

C. FIAT MECHANICS

In the beginning, barter was a method of trade with values determined by a consensus of peers. Over the millennia, came third parties with values determined by brokers and banks. The method of trade also evolved from physical material, such as cowrie shells and salt, to printed paper and minted coins with values backed by gold. That all changed with fiat money, and the best way to characterize fiat is by some of its mechanics including:

1) Fiat value is not backed by anything tangible, but is backed by Government decree and debt at over $20 trillion in the U.S. and over $50 trillion worldwide.

2) Central banks (e.g., the Fed in the U.S.) control monetary policy including how much physical fiat money is to be printed and minted each year by a tax-funded treasury.

3) Central banks make profits several ways including seigniorage tax on fiat sold to banks. Seigniorage is the difference between cost to produce and the face value of the money. For example, in 2019 it cost the U.S. Treasury on average $0.142 to print a $100 bill that was sold to banks at face $100 value -- with a profit at over 70,000%.

4) Banks make profits through fractional reserve lending, meaning that most fiat deposits are not in the bank's vault.

5) Fiat bank account login security is through a login User Identification (ID), strong password, and optional 2-Factor Authentication (2FA).

6) Clearing of transactions between fiat bank accounts takes days through an Automated Clearing House (ACH).

The Tour

7) Fiat settlements between banks use a Real Time Gross Settlements (RTGS) system, and there is an RTGS for each sovereign nation (e.g., Fedwire in the U.S.).

8) Fiat counterfeits are estimated by the U.S. Treasury to be $70 million to $200 million in the U.S., implying possible billions in counterfeits worldwide.

9) Fiat is favored for no risk deposits insured by Federal Deposit Insurance Corporation (FDIC), low to moderate risk investments, public or private legal financial transactions; and private, untraceable **illegal** financial transactions.

10) Fiat alternatives include a variety of printed paper and minted coins controlled by each sovereign nation -- with Dollars in the U.S, Euros in Europe, Rubles in Russia, and so on, along with frequently changing fiat exchange rates.

D. CRYPTO MECHANICS

Before making a comparison with fiat, more knowledge on crypto mechanics would be helpful. Crypto mechanics would include more on wallets, transactions, mining, money creation, making change, volatility, regulation, and recourse for problems.

1) Wallets. Money needs methods for storage, transfer, and security. For fiat there are banks, and for crypto there are wallets. A crypto wallet is a paired public address and private key. Also paired with the private key is a public key used for a digital signature to secure wallet transactions over an insecure Internet. The mathematics of the Elliptic Curve Digital Signature Algorithm (ECDSA) provides the basis for Bitcoin private key and public key pairing, such that a public key can be easily computed from a private key but the reverse is not feasible with computers of today.

The wallet's public address and private key have associated Quick Response (QR) codes for computer and smartphone readability. The public address is like a public mailbox address to receive Bitcoins from anyone. The private key is like a mailbox key that only the owner can use to withdraw Bitcoins. A Bitcoin app on a computer or smartphone can withdraw Bitcoins from a wallet by optically scanning the QR code for the private key. This is referred to as "sweeping" the private key. If the private key is managed by a third party, that third party is the owner of the associated value and operates similar to a bank with a promise to pay on demand.

2) Transactions. Secure transactions between peer wallets are based on the mathematics of Public Key Cryptography (PKC). Peer wallets mean that transactions are between wallets of the same type, such as Bitcoin to Bitcoin or Ethereum to Ethereum, and not between non-peer wallets such as Bitcoin to Ethereum. PKC provides methods to sign a message and verify a transaction.

A signing algorithm produces a digital signature using the message and private key. The digital signature is then verified with the public key that identifies the sender as the owner of the private key and wallet value (without revealing the private key), and that the message and destination public address have not been altered (by a hacker).

An invalid transaction between non-peer wallets, or with an error in content or format between peer wallets, can result in lost value if not detected and rejected before being cleared for entry to the Blockchain. This would be similar to a bad check getting rejected by an Automated Teller Machine (ATM) and not accepted as a fiat deposit. For exchanges between non-peer wallets or between a crypto wallet and fiat bank account, an exchange facility such Coinbase would be used. For that exchange service, there is a fee to cover the costs of the exchange facility's operation.

3) Mining. Money follows technology evolution, with the Internet having a significant impact. Before the Internet, mining was about physical work to find tangible resources. After the Internet, the concept of "mining" expanded to include the work of computers.

Bitcoin first appeared in 2009 as an Internet protocol. That protocol can transfer value between peer wallets and includes a fee-based security service called "mining." Bitcoin mining uses computers (and not picks and shovels) to "clear" valid transactions before entry to the Blockchain. Note that sending Bitcoin to the wrong address can be an error on the part of the sender, possibly resulting in permanent loss of that value if not otherwise rejected as an invalid transaction.

The Blockchain shows "cleared" transactions (i.e., verified, but not in a confirmed block) and "settlements" (i.e., cleared transactions in a confirmed block). It takes about 10 minutes for the first confirmation of a valid block containing about 4,000 Bitcoin transactions.

If a block error is detected by the mining process, there is additional processing for the unconfirmed block with added delay for the transaction settlements.

4) Money Creation. How are new Bitcoins created? In the mining process described previously, miners (or groups in mining pools) must also solve a mathematical challenge. The first to do so is rewarded with new Bitcoins plus mining fees for a confirmed block. The reward is deposited to the winner's wallet as the first transaction in a newly confirmed block.

In the beginning in 2009, that reward was 50 new Bitcoins about every 10 minutes. The reward interval is a protocol parameter, which can vary depending on the Altcoin. For example, Ethereum has a reward interval that varies from 10 to 20 seconds.

In 2019, the reward was 12.5 new Bitcoins about every 10 minutes. Cutting the reward in half is a Bitcoin protocol parameter referred to as "halving" that occurs every 210,000 blocks or about every four years. The next halving will be in May 2020. The last Bitcoin reward will be in 2140, with only mining fees as rewards to continue after 2140. The reward method for Bitcoin is referred to as Proof Of Work (POW). Halving intervals, if any, and alternative methods such as Proof Of Stake (POS), can vary with Altcoins. For example, Ethereum does not have a pre-determined halving interval and is evolving to POS.

The Bitcoin reward reduction is modeled after physical mining. For example, gold mining tends to produce less in time due to the difficulty in finding a reduced supply, but that supply of gold typically has more value. Bitcoin has a similar process with reduced supply and increased value in time. For example, in 2009 Bitcoin had no meaningful value (i.e., crypto dust). In 2010, one Bitcoin was worth less than $1 but has increased to thousands in value over time.

Crypto has mining alternatives. High energy computer facilities are used for mining Bitcoin and Ethereum. A low energy "pre-mined" alternative was used for Ripple (XRP). Pre-mined means there are no miners, and all the crypto is made available in the genesis block, or alternative method depending on the crypto. Mining can result in a distributed process of which miners receive new crypto that is typically labeled as a "currency." Pre-mined crypto is more centralized, and could be labeled as a "security" with implied regulation by the Securities and Exchange Commission (SEC).

5) Making Change. A subtle concept is making change in a crypto transaction. It is similar to making change in a fiat transaction where a customer uses $10 to buy a $2 cup of coffee. The $10 is traded for the coffee and $8 in change. Consider a Bitcoin transaction where a source client wallet1 has 2 Bitcoins and 1 Bitcoin is sent to destination wallet2 to purchase an item. The protocol withdraws the 2 Bitcoins from source client wallet1, sends 1 Bitcoin to destination wallet2 and returns the change (balance less fees) to a new source client wallet3.

That Bitcoin transaction is recorded on the Blockchain as one source (wallet1) and two destinations (wallet2 and wallet3). There are variations in this protocol depending on the Altcoin. For example, with Ethereum (ETH) the source wallet1 would be reduced to a new balance, and there is no new destination wallet3 for change. The Ethereum process was a design choice for simplicity.

6) Volatility. Why so much? Crypto whales (e.g., early adopters and institutional investors) and the law of networks are likely causes. Early adopters were those with mining facilities and first to be rewarded with new crypto, along with those that bought in early for pennies.

The Tour

Institutional investors are recent adopters that manage large financial portfolios. Crypto whales can be responsible for "pump and dump" schemes. They can easily buy large quantities and pump up values, or dump (i.e., sell) and drive down crypto values.

For the law of networks, effects are proportional to the equation $n(n-1)/2$ [i.e., $(n \times (n-1)) / 2$], where n is a function of the number of users and the number of use cases. This equation started with phone networks such that with 1 phone the value would be $1 \times 0/2 = 0$, 2 phones $2 \times 1/2 = 1$, 3 phones $3 \times 2/2 = 3$, 4 phones $4 \times 3/2 = 6$, and so on with exponential increases in value with large n.

Bitcoin started with a few early adopters and now there are millions of users. There is no discrimination in who participates, and it is a way to diversify high risk investments. The base to get started is access to the Internet with a computer or smartphone, along with a crypto exchange account that is linked to a fiat bank account or credit card.

For use cases, there is store of value, investments, day trading, payments, gifts, and exchanges between different types of crypto. For example, Bitcoin can be exchanged with thousands of other Altcoins, through hundreds of crypto exchanges in many countries.

Soon there will be more stablecoins, other than Tether (USDT) and USD Coin (USDC), with values pegged to fiat. New stablecoins can come from sovereign nations, financial organizations, or social networks with billions of users. The law of networks with $n(n-1)/2$ can become exponentially large with a range of values from n(low) = users + use cases to n(high) = users x use cases.

While there is a lower limit to Bitcoin value, there is no higher limit. Changes in Bitcoin's fiat value from less than $0.01 to near $20,000 are part of history. Who is to say that higher values of $100,000 or more will never occur?

Crypto volatility implies significant profit or loss potential. Profits come from buying low and selling high. For the uninformed trying to get rich quick, the result can be a risk of loss by buying high and selling low. For beginners, the best investment is not money but time to learn more about risks and benefits of diversification.

7) Regulation. In the U.S., crypto is regulated more ways than fiat. For fiat, a money services business is required to have a Money Transmitter License (MTL) and comply with Know Your Client (KYC) and Anti-Money Laundering (AML) regulations. A money services business, as defined by Financial Crimes Enforcement Network (FinCEN), can include one or more of several services from currency exchanger to the U.S. Postal Service.

Crypto, however, is regulated four different ways -- as money, property, commodity, and security. Money regulation for crypto is the same as fiat, as specified by FinCEN. Property regulation for crypto is from the Internal Revenue Service (IRS) with guidance that taxes must be paid for crypto profit/loss the same as physical property profit/loss. Commodity regulation is handled by the Commodities Futures Trading Commission (CFTC) that claims a role in emerging crypto innovations. Security regulation was discussed previously where it is possible that pre-mined crypto could be labeled as a "security" and regulated by the SEC.

In time, there will likely be separate regulations for a crypto asset class similar to efforts in Japan. They have the Payment Services Act (PSA) that is scheduled to be effective in 2020. Crypto is used worldwide, with regulations depending on the country, and it is not permitted or illegal where freedoms are restricted.

8) Recourse. What to do if something goes wrong? With fiat banks, deposit accounts have FDIC insurance to protect against a bank's failure. Fiat merchant accounts have purchase, return, repair or replace policies, warranties, loss protection, and a customer service phone number. With crypto, the focus is on prevention. Opening a crypto account may be more complex, but the intent is to prevent the need for recourse. Prevention tools include registration, authentication, accuracy, delay, lockout, and a help desk.

a) Registration for a new account on a crypto exchange begins with a user id, a strong password, and KYC information to determine the allowed level of monetary transactions. The KYC information can include an email address, photo of a driver's license or passport, or a copy of a utility bill.

b) Authentication at login begins with a user id and password, plus optional 2-Factor Authentication (2FA) with entry of a time limited security code from a second source. A test to solve a puzzle, with pictures or patterns, could also be part of authentication to verify that the login is from a person and not a hack attempt from a computer. If the device or computer operating system changes from the original registration, the authentication process could be re-initiated and require 2FA. If the location changes from the original registration, the Internet Service Provider (ISP) could also change and the authentication process could be re-initiated and require 2FA.

c) Accuracy of actions can be checked for format and content with a required response to correct errors or approve the transaction.

d) A delay can occur after all actions are completed, to allow time to make further changes or to cancel the transaction.

e) Lockout can occur if there are too many login errors or the authentication process must be re-initiated too many times.

f) The help desk can be contacted for guidance or the next steps to fix a lockout for a registered user, with unregistered users or hackers getting blocked from entry.

E. COMPARISON: CRYPTO vs. FIAT

Crypto and fiat mechanics have significant differences. This section considers several areas including value, production, storage, transport, security, seigniorage, fractional reserves, account logins, clearing, settlements, counterfeits, and financial transactions:

1) Crypto value is determined by a world marketplace vs. fiat value that is determined by Government decree.

2) Crypto's digital creation and distribution has time and cost savings vs. fiat's tax-funded physical production, storage, transport, and security for printed paper and minted coins.

3) Crypto can have transaction fees, but no hidden seigniorage tax with huge markups in fiat money sold to banks.

4) Crypto wallets store all the value while fiat banks, with fractional reserve lending, do not store all the deposits in the bank's vault.

5) Crypto exchange login security is similar to fiat bank accounts with user id's, strong passwords, and 2FA, but wallets have the additional cryptographic security of private keys that can be passphrase protected.

6) Miners clear crypto transactions for entry to the blockchain in minutes vs. fiat's ACH that takes days.

7) There is a separate blockchain for worldwide settlements for each type of crypto vs. fiat with a separate costly RTGS for each sovereign nation, while the blockchain and RTGS provide common one-way, irreversible transactions.

8) Crypto is designed to prevent double spends that would be similar to preventing counterfeits of fiat money with possibly billions of counterfeits worldwide.

9) Crypto is favored for diversification for high-risk financial investments and USDC that pays interest (e.g., 1.25% at Coinbase), but is **not** favored for private, untraceable illegal financial transactions as in fiat, since wallet transactions on the blockchain/DLT are traceable.

10) Crypto can be used worldwide vs. fiat that is specific to a sovereign nation. Crypto also has variety. Some crypto have volatile market values, while others have stable values pegged to stable assets.

Selected crypto in this book represent evolving technologies. Classifications are for education and not investment advice. Main classification is by nth Generation (nG) for comparison of different accounting ledgers and transaction verification methods.

1G-3G crypto has blockchain-based ledgers with miners providing transaction verification, and includes 1G Bitcoin (BTC), 2G Ethereum (ETH), and 3G Cardano (ADA).

4G-6G crypto has a variety of DLT with transaction verification that is typically referred to as Fast, Fee-less and Miner-less (FFM). FFM crypto includes 4G IOTA (MIOTA), 5G Nano (NANO) and Holo (HOT), and 6G Bitlattice.

Now for more on what is beyond blockchain.

F. BEYOND BLOCKCHAIN

Topics include Internet Of Things (IOT), bank and social networks, sovereignty, trace to verified source, and modern economies.

1) Internet Of Things. With the Internet and wireless creating a new communications paradigm, IOT will have a new mystery -- electronic transactions between things with identities. The mechanics of IOT will come with 4G-6G crypto.

4G IOTA has transaction verification via clients vs. miners, and single-entry Transaction ID (1xTXID) accounting. Verification will be with secure client software, similar to free https browsing. With 1xTXID, clients settle their own transactions by verifying two previous transactions, with a settlement record on the Directed Acyclic Graph (DAG)-based Tangle DLT.

5G crypto, such as Nano and Holo, have transaction verification via clients vs. miners, with double-entry Transaction ID (2xTXID) accounting. Double-entry means there are separate transactions for clearing (i.e., a send or debit transaction) and settlement (i.e, a receive or credit transaction). Nano uses a DAG Block Lattice for parallel client processing with each client on a separate DLT. Nano provides a scalable and secure foundation for financial transactions that can compete with Bitcoin. Holo uses a Distributed Hash Table (DHT) for parallel client processing with each client on a separate hash table DLT. Holo provides a scalable and secure foundation for applications and smart contracts that can compete with Ethereum.

6G Bitlattice will provide a multi-dimensional system for distributed data storage and processing. Details are limited with updates at *jmwnuk.wixsite.com/digitalassets/beyond-blockchain*.

2) Bank and Social Networks. With billions of worldwide users, bank and social networks are creating new stablecoins with new methods for clearing and settlements.

The Tour

Their efforts can challenge banks with aging ACH and RTGS systems. Social networks can be competition for credit brands. Credit cards are in use 24/7 worldwide for shopping, restaurants, entertainment, and travel. Bank and social networks can modernize such that:

a) Fiat money is diversified with crypto such as Bitcoin and Ethereum, and stablecoins such as USDT, USDC, J.P. Morgan (JPM) Coin, and Facebook's Libra.

b) Fiat banks with RTGS's can diversify with modern settlements such as the Quorum DLT for the JPM Coin.

c) Fiat credit brands can diversify with Facebook's Calibra financial services wallet on a smartphone.

3) Sovereignty. China has banned cryptocurrencies. At one time they had many traders and miners. What happened? With crypto it was too easy to move money out of China. That lack of control threatened sovereignty. China understood the value of crypto, but needed better control of money flow. Their solution will likely be a sovereign stablecoin. Mu Changchun, a deputy director in the People's Bank of China (PBOC), is leading the effort for a sovereign crypto. That sovereign crypto would likely have value by decree, scalable capacity, with an added layer for a reputation ratings. That rating would be more than a FICO® Score, and people and businesses could be rewarded (or punished) based on their rating.

4) Trace to Verified Source. Source is the beginning (i.e., genesis) of something of value. The genesis block in a blockchain or DLT is the first block. The chain means that every block, after the genesis block, references a previous block. That reference uses a hash function to verify that a transaction has not been altered and can trace to a verified source. That trace to an unaltered and verified source is what allows transactions to be cleared and settled on a blockchain or DLT.

For crypto, the blockchain/DLT process verifies transactions with financial value. That concept can also be used for non-financial applications – similar to United Parcel Service (UPS) tracking parcels. Enhanced with status data, the "on-chain" process can track: changes of ownership in title transactions, quality of parts used in construction transactions, conditions for food transactions from farm to grocery store, medicine transactions from ingredients and formulas to pharmacy products, and so on.

Many organizations are providing education and building on-chain systems for tracking in non-financial applications. They include at least: Amazon, Deloitte, Harvard, International Business Machines (IBM), Microsoft, Massachusetts Institute of Technology (MIT), and Oracle.

5) Modern Economies. Modern economies have off-chain and on-chain components. Off-chain includes systems with transactions that are not on a blockchain/DLT. Off-chain transactions can include those at home for lifestyle, healthcare and welfare; and what's trending for income, rewards and payments. Off-chain also includes existing financial systems for banking, investments and insurance; and a nation's transactions for its treasury and handling of assets and liabilities.

On-chain includes systems with transactions that are on a blockchain/DLT (1G-3G) or DLT/FFM (4G-6G). On-chain systems include crypto exchanges, crypto wallets and crypto mining. Of particular interest are off-chain to on-chain trends for flexible income, rewards, and payments. A traditional plastic credit/debit card, modernized with an on-chain QR code could have worldwide use. That plastic card would not require power or communications as in a computer or smartphone, but could be used by anyone at anyplace that has power and communications.

Trending use cases for flexible income, rewards and payments include:

a) Income from payroll, social security, or welfare, can be deposited to crypto public address represented by a QR code on a modern debit card. That income can be sent by the corresponding on-chain organization. The recipient could choose if and when the crypto value is exchanged to a fiat value for traditional use with a modern debit card.

b) Rewards from shopping, dining, entertainment, or travel can be deposited with process similar to a) above with value sent by the corresponding rewarding on-chain organization. The recipient's rewards card would operate as a modern debit card as in a) above.

c) Payments for travel and credit cards is defined in patent US10204378B1. When it is time to pay credit card charges, with this patent the consumer can make payments with money with best value — either (off-chain) fiat or (on-chain) crypto.

With availability of off-chain and on-chain capabilities, users can choose which has the best benefits. For example, fiat purchases with a credit card has advantages at the point of sale with transactions confirmed in seconds. When it is time to pay those credit card charges, the best benefit would be a choice to pay with money with best value — either fiat or crypto.

The words above can be used to create many pictures. One picture is Figure 1 on Modern Economies as shown on the next page. The level of integration of off-chain and on-chain depends on the level of diversity in a nation's economy. More about Figure 1 is in Section G (New Choices) and Section H (New Foundations).

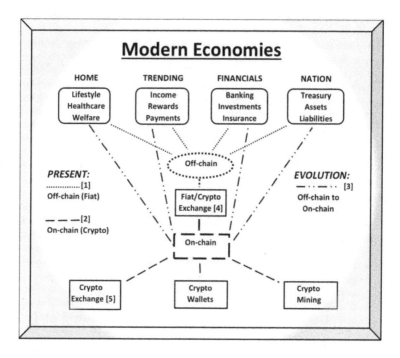

Figure 1.

[1] **Off-chain**: Transaction are not recorded on a blockchain or DLT.

[2] **On-chain**: Transactions are recorded on a blockchain or DLT.

[3] **Evolution: Off-chain to On-chain**: An off-chain economy can modernize by diversifying with on-chain capabilities.

[4] **Fiat/Crypto Exchange**: An exchange, such as Coinbase or BitTrex, that has fee-based capability to receive, store, and withdraw or exchange between fiat and crypto.

[5] **Crypto Exchange**: An exchange such as Binance, that has fee-based capability to receive, store, and withdraw crypto, and exchange between different types of crypto, but does not have fiat capability.

G. NEW CHOICES

"The future is not what it used to be." An interesting quote attributed to several persons including Yogi Berra, Paul Valery, and others. As shown in Figure 1, off-chain was the world economies before crypto. Off-chain progress continues with more choices ahead for: communications, trade and money processes.

1) Off-Chain Progress. Observables in a communications system can be compared with an iceberg. The tip of the iceberg is visible but most is unseen and below the water. In communications, what starts as the tip with voice, data, or video on visible devices such as a phone, computer or TV, quickly becomes unseen bits passing over unseen physical facilities. These facilities could include: modems, Wi-Fi routers, coax and fiber cables, multiplexing hubs, cellular antennas, Telco central office, Internet Service Provider (ISP), and then on to a destination or access to the World Wide Web (WWW).

Progress in mobile wireless communications has evolved over several decades from 1G Analog with poor quality and dropped calls, to digital with high quality and performance. Digital technology included 2G Time Division Multiple Access (TDMA) with the signal on one frequency that is time slotted to serve multiple users, to 3G Code Division Multiple Access (CDMA) with more security, to modern Orthogonal Frequency Division Multiplexing (OFDM) with the signal carried on multiple frequencies that are time slotted for more users and higher speeds. OFDM is the current technology for Wi-Fi, 4G mobile wireless, new deployments of 5G mobile wireless, and planned future deployments of 6G mobile wireless communications.

Scalability for growing and changing load conditions in wired and mobile wireless have come from the technical innovation of a Recursive Inter-Network Architecture (RINA).

The Tour

A basic premise of RINA is that networking is inter-process communications (IPC) and different systems can communicate and share data using a Distributed IPC Facility (DIF). Many services depend on communications. No dial tone or an Internet outage is a wakeup call to the value of those services, as it becomes necessary to adapt to life without instant communications.

Income is one of many off-chain services that depends on communications. Income can be from several sources including: work, investments, social security, or welfare. Deposits go to an online bank account, with off-chain foundations for that money flow based on unseen ACH and RTGS. Credit and debit cards are part of the accepted norm to simplify purchases with almost instant checkout at the point of sale. Credit card payments are made easy using a computer or smartphone with Wi-Fi access to the Internet.

While many like the idea of having pocket money for shopping, most fiat money transactions are not with tangible cash but with an on-line Internet purchase, or at a store with a credit/debit card. When benefits of on-chain innovations become known, that can be the incentive for their adoption. The on-chain innovation started the crypto era that provided a new perspective on how the future could be very different from what it used to be.

2) On-Chain Innovations. On-chain first appeared in 2009 with a Bitcoin value layer on the Internet. It bypassed banks and costly delays of cross-border wire transfers. After a decade of growth, industry and governments see the benefits of on-chain methods for financial and non-financial applications. Benefits of on-chain include performance (e.g., clearing in minutes vs. days for ACH), security (e.g., cryptography vs. passwords), reduced costs (e.g., pennies for crypto transaction fees vs. dollars for fiat wire transfers), and double spend or counterfeit prevention for crypto but not fiat.

The Tour

The underlying foundations for on-chain crypto methods are also unseen (or poorly understood), but crypto and distributed ledgers are part of ongoing worldwide transformation and diversification. To make on-chain financial applications more like off-chain methods, volatile crypto is morphing into stablecoins with values tied to fiat (debt-based) money. For non-financial applications, on-chain methods can provide improvements to supply chains.

A supply chain is the production and delivery methods to make a product or to provide a service. Tracking of parts can follow a variety of off-chain methods, and tracing back to sources is not likely a part of the process — unless defects or disasters occur. The variety of methods for tracking and tracing will likely be unified with on-chain methods for food, gems, minerals, medicine, equipment, news, photoshopping, and IDs.

If a food product is bad and removed from store shelves, and the process from production to delivery is tracked, quick identification of the source of defects can result in timely repair of process. Considering coffee, it would be important to know if expensive coffee came from the claimed legal source that was environmentally friendly and not full-sun coffee beans.

If the source of gems was traced to blood diamonds, that tracing could result in reduced sales and/or improved conditions for production without child labor. The same could apply for the new blood mineral cobalt. Cobalt is used in jet engine alloys, as a medical tracer in radiotherapy for cancer, and now has greatest use in lithium batteries for smartphones, computers and electric vehicles.

If a medicine is defective and causes injury or death, tracing back to sources can enable the understanding of the cause of the defect to be followed by ingredient or formula improvements. If brakes or other equipment on a vehicle are defective, fast tracing to sources and quick repair or replacement can save lives.

The Tour

News is data that is an essential part of an economy. News that is not based on facts, but on biased opinions or false witness such as in the Kavanaugh hearings, can lead to bad choices for a misinformed public and businesses. Bad choices can eventually lead to disaster for an economy. Fact-based news that can be traced to verified sources will likely be part of modern healthy economies.

Photoshopping is altering a digital image. Popular uses include taking out age marks to improve appearance, retouching old photos to make them look like new, or adding color to a black and white image. Instructional videos show how to change the digital image of a person from thin to buff, or brunette to redhead, and so on. The darkside is that easy digital editing has been used for false advertising. An example would be a famous person falsely shown as endorsing a diet pill or brain-boosting pill. With modern tracking methods, digital images can have digital tracking of time, place and serial number of software that made the edit. Consumers can then be warned when an original image has been altered.

IDs for people are important for licenses, travel, credit, security clearances, voting, and more. Imagine what would happen to a nation if anyone could vote with a fake ID. Proof of ID with traceability to a verified source has become the norm. In the future, IDs traced to verified birth date, time, location, parents, and more, will likely be part of modern healthy economies.

Making a choice to diversify with what is new can be a slow process. It took decades for the value of the (off-chain) Internet to be understood. With time and cost benefits of the Internet, use has become an accepted norm for mail, messages, wireless phone calls, streaming TV, web browsing, social networking, and on-line purchases and payments. In a similar way, understanding new on-chain methods and their foundations can give insight to potential new benefits in financial and non-financial applications.

H. NEW FOUNDATIONS

What follows is more on new foundations for the on-chain world to include: forks in the road, scalable capacity, quantum security, and importance of learning from dark and bright sides of history.

1) Forks in the Road. On-chain protocols have public roadmaps for modernization plans. Private roadmaps can also exist when considering competition. Roadmaps include strategy, tactics, and schedules. Points in time for planned upgrades are called "forks." Planned forks can be for new features, improved scalability or to reduce operational costs. Unplanned forks can also occur for urgent protocol changes to repair defects.

Forks are classified as hard or soft. Hard forks are for major changes where miners or developers disagree on how to proceed. Hard forks can result in a splitting the main chain, such that a new secondary chain is created. That secondary chain typically has only forward compatibility from the time of the fork, and results in a new cryptocurrency for the secondary chain. Soft forks are for minor changes where the majority agree to make the change. Soft forks do not result in splitting the main chain or a new cryptocurrency.

An example of a classic hard fork was ETH to Ethereum Classic (ETC) on July 20,2016. The hard fork was due to a Distributed Autonomous Organization (DAO) coding error and the hack was first observed on June 18, 2016. DAO was a smart contract built on the Ethereum platform. The ETH fix was to update the original errored DAO code with another DAO smart contract that only had a "withdraw" function. The purpose of the withdraw function was to allow original owners to withdraw their hacked ETH funds. Some miners, however, disagreed with the main ETH approach for "justice" and wanted "truth" by retaining the "immutable" characteristic of a cryptocurrency.

The Tour

Those disagreeing miners initiated the hard fork to the secondary ETC chain on July 20, 2016 at ETH block 1920000. Both ETH and ETC start with the same genesis block, but ETH now has the corrected DAO code and ETC retained the errored DAO code. On the positive side, owners of ETH before the DAO hack, gained an equal number of ETC. Today, ETH and ETC have independent and volatile values based on market conditions, with transactions recorded on separate ETH and ETC blockchains.

Another classic hard fork was with BTC and Bitcoin Cash (BCH) that took place in August 1, 2017. A group of BTC developers wanted to improve performance by increasing the block size limit. That effort divided the Bitcoin community such that BCH with an increased block size was able to processes transactions faster than BTC. The BTC main chain is backward compatible to the first genesis block in 2009. BCH is on a secondary chain that started on August 1, 2017 and is not backward compatible to the BTC genesis block. The good news was that those that held BTC at the time of the fork received an equal number of BCH. If you held 10 BTC on August 1, 2017, on August 2, 2017 you would have 10 BTC plus 10 BCH. BTC and BCH have independent and volatile values based on market conditions, with transactions recorded on separate BTC and BCH blockchains.

2) Scalable Capacity. Scalability becomes essential for sustainable clearing and settlements in financial transactions, and tracking and tracing in non-financial transactions. Scalability must also address trade-offs with security and decentralization. Early Bitcoin and Ethereum protocols did not have scalable capacity for clearing and settlements. Crypto is great for store of value, but is too slow at the point of sale compared to credit/debit cards.

Miners worldwide have a severe bottleneck when they try to get their transactions on-chain. Less than 10 transactions a second (tps) for Bitcoin and slightly more for Ethereum will never be able to compete with more than 1,000 tps with credit and debit cards.

The Tour

The year 2020 will likely be the start for significant improvements in scalable capacity with: lightning networks, sharding, RINA, epochs, and client verification.

a) The Lightning Network is intended to provide scalable capacity for Bitcoin. It was suggested by Thaddeus Dryja and Joseph Poon in January 14, 2016, and code development is part of BIP0068 and BIP0112. An off-chain (or side-chain) payment channel between peer users will start and end with on-chain transactions that are part of a smart Hashed Timelock Contract (HTLC). FFM off-chain transactions will be allowed while the payment channel is open.

For security, the smart HTLC will require Bitcoin deposits for the payment channel setup. If one of the users becomes a bad actor (i.e., scammer, hacker) and does not honor the smart contract, their deposit will be withdrawn and given to the other peer user.

The idea is to stop hacking attempts when the cost of a hack would far exceeds any possible return. Some of the features in the Lightning Network proposal include: rapid payments, no third-party, reduced blockchain load, and channels stay open indefinitely. More details are at *en.bitcoin.it/wiki/Lightning_Network*.

b) Sharding is the Ethereum approach to scalability. A blockchain database would be split into several parts called "shards", with parallel processing in each shard as the key to scalability. Sharding is expected to be implemented as part of Ethereum 2.0 starting in 2020 with six phases corresponding to soft forks including: basic sharding, state transition, light client, cross-shard transactions, tight coupling, and exponential sharding. Details for each phase can be found at *github.com/ethereum/wiki/wiki/Sharding-roadmap*.

c) Scalability in Cardano will follow techniques similar to what was perfected in mobile wireless communications including: RINA, TDMA and OFDM. To handle a large and growing number of transactions, Cardano splits the network into smaller "subnetworks" using a RINA technique. Each node can become part of a subnetwork and communicate with other nodes in other subnets.

Examples of use of RINA in mobile wireless communications would be a large stadium with thousands watching a sporting or entertainment event. Spectators with smartphones could be texting, talking and streaming video to others worldwide. How all that works with fast setup and take down of capacity is RINA technology, and Cardano is bringing RINA-like implementation to the world of cryptocurrencies.

Epochs in Cardano are similar to TDMA and OFDM perfected in mobile wireless communications. Time in Cardano is divided into epochs. Every epoch is divided into slots. Every 20 seconds there is a slot and an epoch contains 21,600 slots to represent exactly five days. For scalability, the number of slots per epoch can be changed and there can be parallel epochs. In comparison with mobile wireless, operation with one epoch is like TDMA and operation with parallel epochs is like OFDM. More on Cardano scalability can be found at *cardanoroadmap.com/en/basho/*.

d) Scalability in IOTA will be achieved with client verification of transactions vs. miner verification. As the number of client users increases so does the verification capacity. The technique for transaction verification is based on DAG and Coordicide. In DAG, the letter "D" (i.e., Directed) implies a start and end point, such as a destination in navigation or source of value in a financial transaction, "A" (i.e., Acyclic) means the start and end routing cannot get stuck in an endless cyclic pattern, and "G" (i.e., Graph) is a popular part of mathematics finding a modern use in crypto applications.

Coordicide is the decentralized version of IOTA's older centralized coordinator. It provides scalability in terms of transactions per second, and has the ability to create smart contracts. The whitepaper is at *files.iota.org/papers/Coordicide_WP.pdf,* and there is an interesting visual model of the IOTA DLT at *tangle.glumb.de/.*

3) Quantum Security. On-chain foundations must be tolerant to the threat of quantum computers attempting to decode private keys. Quantum computers are the new age of super computers rated in quantum bits (qubits). In classical computers, each bit can be in one of two states — on or off, or 0 or 1. In quantum computers, probabilities come in to play, such that a theoretical qubit can have more than two states. In general, a qubit rating = 1 implies capability of present computers, quibit = 2 implies capability 4x present computers, and so on. A rating of n implies 2^n capability over present computers.

Current claims are qubit ratings near 50 from IBM and Google, and 2,000 from D-Wave Systems, Inc. One hopes that this powerful qubit capability is used to decode causes of cancer, alzheimers and other diseases; and not decoding of private keys or logins and passwords to steal from financial accounts.

Crypto professionals have a variety of security methods that are tolerant to hack attempts from quantum computers. In the years 2020 and later there will likely be enhanced quantum security. Methods for quantum security include: elliptic curves, sponge construction, Hierarchical Deterministic (HD) wallets, and more advances in Public Key Cryptography (PKC) as follows:

a) PKC with ECDSA, secp256k1's elliptic curve $y^2 = x^3 + 7$, and SHA-256 hash is used in Bitcoin Wallets. Quantum hackers focus on ECDSA as it is a National Security Agency (NSA) standard, with decode of the private key estimated by 2030 or earlier.

The Tour

b) PKC with ECDSA, secp256k1 and the Keccak-256 hash based on sponge construction is not an NSA standard and is used in Ethereum Wallets. Sponge-based construction can compress or expand a bit stream by taking an input bit stream of any length and produce an output bit stream with a desired length.

c) PKC with EdDSA, elliptic Curve25519 (Ed25519) and SHA-512 hash is not an NSA standard and is used by Nano and Holo and in Cardano's HD Daedalus Wallet. Daedakus is Cardano's wallet for the ADA cryptocurrency. Use of Ed25519 and HD Wallets, hides the wallet that has value and could add years or decades to private key decode time by quantum hackers.

d) PKC with a Winternitz DSA and Troika hash is used in IOTA's Trinity Wallet. The Troika hash, based on sponge construction, was designed by CYBERCRYPT to tolerate all known attacks from crypto and quantum hackers. The (Robert) Winternitz DSA builds on the work of Leslie Lamport and Ralph Merkle, and groups w bits to be signed with n groups for each wallet. With this approach, the user can vary w and n in time to make speed or storage the priority depending on load conditions and security objectives.

e) Crypto exchanges also hide the wallet with value with Exchange wallets. Value is moved from an owner's on-chain electronic wallet to an Exchange wallet. An exchange, such as Coinbase, also offers off-chain "vault" services for added security. A withdrawal from a vault requires 2FA, two co-signers to approve the withdrawal, and a 48 hour delay before the withdrawal occurs.

There will be many ways to foil quantum hackers. One wonders if it would ever be possible for the quantum hacker to decode a private key or hack a financial account? Their time and effort and possible tax money for development, would have more value if used to decode causes and cure diseases, poverty, hunger and illiteracy.

4) Abraxas. No tour of the evolution of trade and money can be complete without a review of dark and bright sides. It is important to learn from both -- to leverage the bright side and not repeat the dark side. The dark side of crypto has included: Mt. Gox, Silk Road, and a possible 51% attack.

Mt. Gox was a crypto exchange that went bankrupt as a result of thousands of Bitcoins being hacked. It is an example of what can happen when a crypto exchange is poorly managed and does not follow sound financial practice that is as good as or better than banks. Silk Road was a crypto operation that allowed transactions of illegal products. The darker side of Silk Road was that the investigating government agents were stealing confiscated Bitcoins. More on the history of Mt. Gox and the Silk Road court cases is found in the References: Dark Side.

A 51% attack could destroy a crypto system (or a democracy). A 51% crypto attack occurs when a mining pool controls more than 50% of mining resources. Dark side impacts could include transactions not getting confirmed and confirmed transactions getting reversed. Self monitoring has been the prevention approach. By observing a possible 51% attack, the crypto community can take corrective action if necessary. Actions could include protocol improvements, corrective smart contracts, or black listing the offending mining operation.

For comparison of a 51% attack with a democracy, consider the U.S. Electoral system as a smart contract that arbitrates between "justice" and "truth" in an election. The Electoral system can provide fairness (justice) by preventing a popular vote (truth) from a clustered 51% of voters in a few cities from taking control of a nation with over 19,000 cities, towns, villages, and boroughs.

The Tour

On the bright side, there are many examples. First is the growth of crypto from Bitcoin in 2009 to thousands of Altcoins in 2020 with billions in value. Clearing and settlements with crypto are more economic, faster and more secure than fiat.

Verifiability, that comes with crypto financial applications, can make money laundering a thing of the past with traceability to verified sources. But recall from comparison 9) on page 16, that because of untraceability, fiat will likely be the choice for criminal money laundering and shell operations such as described in *www.youtube.com/watch?v=SedvMc1bdJs*.

Traceability to verified sources will have application in non-financial applications. Trace to source of defective foods, parts, medicines will allow quick repair and replacement with priceless health and safety benefits.

Sustainability becomes evident with crypto and DLT that are effective and efficient. The modern era will include 4G-6G crypto (and communications) that are essential foundations for IOT, AI, and quantum computing.

There are reviews of wallets and exchanges to help make informed choices. Informed choices can also result from the advice of legal, fiduciary and tax professionals. And check the Glossary to be more informed about meaning of abbreviations and terms.

Read *Blocky explains Blockchain* and then read it to your grandchildren. If you have a unique story to tell, do it and self-publish. Instructions from publishers are in the References to help get that important book started.

Live long, be happy.

References

The Tour
The Tour 1st Edition:
www.amazon.com/dp/0578568659
The Tour 2nd Edition:
www.amazon.com/dp/0578613174
The Tour 2nd Edition eBOOK pdf with hotlink references:
jmwnuk.wixsite.com/digitalassets/the-tour-2nd-edition
Earlier version of *The Tour* is in the *4 M's eBOOK CHAPTER I*:
linkedin.com/pulse/money-book-john-wnuk
Risks and Disclosure:
jmwnuk.wixsite.com/digitalassets/disclaimer

More on Fiat and Crypto Mechanics
Modern Money Mechanics (fiat money) by the Federal Reserve:
upload.wikimedia.org/wikipedia/commons/4/4a/Modern_Money_Mechanics.pdf
World Debt Clock (for fiat money):
www.usdebtclock.org/world-debt-clock.html
Fiat is Preferred over Crypto for Money Laundering:
www.tap.global/fiat-used-money-laundering-800x-crypto
Crypto values and status data in Coin Market Capitalizations:
coinmarketcap.com/
Exchange reviews:
steemit.com/cryptocurrency/@singhisking1/best-cryptocurrency-exchanges-in-2020-get-ready
Wallet reviews:
www.thebalance.com/best-bitcoin-wallets-4160642
Paper Wallet generator:
walletgenerator.net/#

The Tour

Dark Side

Mt. Gox heyday, bankruptcy, rehabilitation, and more: *techcrunch.com/2019/02/06/the-plot-to-revive-mt-gox-and-repay-victims-bitcoin/*

Silk Road Court Case against Ulbricht (aka Dread Pirate Roberts): *caselaw.findlaw.com/us-2nd-circuit/1862572.html*

Silk Road Court Case against Agents Force and Bridges: *www.justice.gov/sites/default/files/opa/press-releases/attachments/2015/03/30/criminal_complaint_force.pdf*

Monitored Mining Pools to prevent a 51% attack: *www.blockchain.com/pools?timespan=4days*

Bright Side

Blockchain use cases: *builtin.com/blockchain/blockchain-applications*

Blocky explains Blockchain – A kids' book about the blockchain: *www.amazon.com/dp/1775324222*

Beyond Blockchain for the IOT, AI, and quantum era*: jmwnuk.wixsite.com/digitalassets/beyond-blockchain*

Instructions to self-publish a book on a favorite topic:
> *kdp.amazon.com/en_US/*
> *www.archwaypublishing.com/*
> *www.bowker.com/products/Self-Publishing-Solutions.html*

Glossary

1G ... nG: 1st ... n^{th} Generation. Crypto as in blockchain-based: 1G Bitcoin, 2G Ethereum, 3G Cardano; or FFM: 4G IOTA, 5G Nano and Holo, and 6G Bitlattice; or as in mobile wireless communications: 1G Analog, 2G TDMA, 3G CDMA, 4G/5G/6G OFDM evolution.
1xTXID: Single-entry Transaction ID accounting.
2FA: 2-Factor Authentication.
2xTXID: Double-entry Transaction ID accounting.
4 M's: Mysteries of Modern Money Mechanics.

Abraxas: A mystic god/devil representing good/evil, bright/dark, pro/con, love/hate, kind/mean, order/chaos, honest/corrupt, ...
ACH: Automated Clearing House.
ADA: A 3G mined cryptocurrency with market value and transactions recorded on the scalable Cardano blockchain. Founder was Charles Hoskinson.
AI: Augmented Intelligence for a person. Artificial Intelligence for a device, robot, or computer.
Altcoin: Cryptocurrency other than Bitcoin with market value.
AML: Anti-Money Laundering.
ATM: Automated Teller Machine.

Bankruptcy: Chapter 7: Debtor must sell off nonexempt assets to pay creditors; Chapter 13: As part of reorganization, debtor must provide substantial pay back to creditors within three to five years.
BCH: Bitcoin Cash. A mined cryptocurrency with market value and transactions recorded on the BCH blockchain.
BIP: Bitcoin Improvement Proposal.
BIP0032: Standard for Hierarchical Deterministic (HD) Wallets, with a hierarchical tree-like structure for private/public key pairs.
BIP0038: Encrypts the private key on a paper wallet with a passphrase for more security if the wallet is lost or stolen.
BIP0068/0112/0113: Used in the smart contract in Bitcoin's Lightning Network.

Bitcoin Wallet: Paired public address and private key for the BTC cryptocurrency.

Bitlattice. A novel 6G DLT for distributed data storage and processing. Founder was Hibryda.

block: Group of transactions on a blockchain.

Blockchain: Permanent, distributed, digital, public ledger of worldwide Bitcoin transactions. Lower case "blockchain" or DLT in this book is used for the public ledger of Altcoin transactions.

BTC: Bitcoin. A peer-to-peer Electronic Cash System. A 1G mined cryptocurrency with market value and transactions recorded on the BTC Blockchain. Founder was Satoshi Nakamoto.

Calibra: Digital wallet for Facebook's Libra cryptocurrency.

Cardano: A blockchain for the ADA cryptocurrency. Founder was Charles Hoskinson

CDMA: Code Division Multiple Access. A 3G mobile wireless communications technology.

CFTC: Commodities Futures Trading Commission.

chain: Links in a blockchain/DLT based on a hash function that allows transactions to trace back to verified sources (or genesis).

clearing: When a crypto transaction is verified and added to an unconfirmed block. Compare with fiat clearing with ACH.

cold storage: Cryptocurrency on media that does not connect to the Internet.

confirmed block: A block in a blockchain or DLT that has not been rejected due to errors or altering of transaction content.

counterfeit: Fraudulent imitation of something of value such as fraudulent forging of fiat money.

coupon: Term used by Holo for their ERC-20 cryptocurrency.

CPA: Certified Public Accountant. An accounting and tax professional who has met additional certification requirements.

crypto: Short form of cryptocurrency.

cryptocurrency: Money based on cryptographic methods.

cryptography: Methods for secure communications in the presence of unfriendly third parties.

CYBERCRYPT: Provider of robust cryptography. Developed the Troika hash function for IOTA's DAG architecture and Trinity wallet.

D-Wave Systems, Inc: A quantum computing company based in Canada.

DAG: Directed Acyclic Graph. Use of graph theory to trace transaction data to a verified source.

DAO: Distributed Autonomous Organization. A decentralized organization of computers not controlled by a government or bank.

decree: An official order by a legal authority.

DHT: Distributed Hash Table as used in 5G Holo (HOT).

DIF: Distributed IPC Facility. A single repeating layer in RINA that allows rapid response to changing loads in mobile communications.

digital: A binary sequence of 0's and 1's in computers that represents data.

digital signature: Method to sign a message with a private key without revealing the private key.

DLT: Distributed Ledger Technology.

double spend: A flaw in a money system so that money can be spent more than once as in counterfeit fiat money.

ECDSA: Elliptic Curve Digital Signature Algorithm. Method to compute a public key from a private key such that the reverse computation is not feasible, and to digitally sign a message with a private key without revealing that private key.

EdDSA: Edwards-curve Digital Signature Algorithm. Designed to be faster than ECDSA without sacrificing security.

Ed25519: Digital signing using EdDSA and encryption with elliptic Curve25519. Used in Cardano's HD Daedalus Wallet, Nano and Holo. Curve25519 was designed for TLS v1.3.

Electoral System: Each state in the U.S. gets a number of electors based on number of representatives in Congress. Electors cast one electoral vote following the general election and there are a total of 538 electoral votes. The candidate that gets more than half (270 or more) wins the election.

Electronic Cash System: Bitcoin. A protocol on the Internet for transfer of value between peers, with worldwide transactions recorded on a public Blockchain.

elliptic curve: Curve or plot points on a graph based on the equation $y^2 = x^3 + ax + b$. For Bitcoin and Ethereum cryptocurrencies, a = 0 and b = 7.

Epoch: Method of dividing time the blockchain in the Cardano Settlement Layer. Epochs are divided into slots. Epochs and slots are numbered such that slot (2,7) is "second epoch, seventh slot."

ERC-20 token: Cryptocurrency designed for the Ethereum platform.

ETC: Ethereum Classic. A mined cryptocurrency with market value and transactions recorded on the ETC blockchain.

ETH: Ethereum. A 2G mined cryptocurrency with market value and transactions recorded on a programmable Ethereum blockchain. Co-founders were Vitalik Buterin, Anthony Di Iorio, Charles Hoskinson, Mihai Alisie, and Amir Chetrit.

Exchange Wallet: A wallet used by an exchange such as Coinbase, to add more security to a user's electronic wallet.

Facebook: An online social network where people create profiles, share information, and respond to information posted by others.

FDIC: Federal Deposit Insurance Corporation.

Fed: Federal Reserve System. The central bank for the U.S.

Fee-less transaction: Method of transaction verification that does not require miners or their costs.

FFM: Fast, Fee-less, and Miner-less as in 4G-6G crypto.

fiat: Money with value based on a government decree and not based on a tangible commodity such as gold.

FICO® Score: Credit rating by Fair Isaac Corporation. Score <580 is poor, 580-799 is fair to very good, and 800+ is exceptional.

FinCEN: Financial Crimes Enforcement Network.

forks: Planned enhancements or maintenance points in a cryptocurrency development roadmap.

Fractional Reserve Lending: Bank deposits are lent to others to generate interest income and are not stored in a bank vault.

genesis: The source or origin of something of value. The first block in a blockchain.

gold standard: Monetary system where a country's paper money can be converted to a fixed amount of gold.

halving: A point in time when a block reward is cut in half.

hard fork: Change in a blockchain or DLT to include a secondary chain.

hash: Method to compute a fixed length text from a message of any length, and used to identify if a message has been altered.

HD Wallet: Hierarchical Deterministic Wallet. A system for deriving private-public key pairs from a starting seed as defined in BIP0032.

heyday: Time or phase of greatest prosperity, success, or vigor.

HOT: Holo: A 5G pre-mined cryptocurrency with market values. Each client maintains a private chain managed with a DHT. Uses double-entry Transaction ID (2xTXID) mutual-credit accounting with separate debit and credit transactions. Founder was Arthur Brock.

HTLC: Hashed Timelock Contract. Proposal for Bitcoin's Lightning Network to improve scalability.

http: hyper text transfer protocol for non-secure Internet browsing.

https: http secure: Uses Secure Socket Layer (SSL) or Transport Layer Security (TSL) as a sublayer under http.

IBM: International Business Machines.

ID: Identification.

IEEE 802.11: Institute of Electronic and Electrical Engineers standard 802.11. Part of the IEEE 802 set of Local Area Network (LAN) protocols for Wi-Fi computer communications.

immutable: Not changing, or unable to be changed.

Internet: Worldwide network of computers and standard protocols to route packets of data and provide access to information.

IOT: Internet Of Things.

IOTA: A 4G pre-mined cryptocurrency with market value and single-entry transaction Transaction ID (1xTXID) accounting on the scalable Tangle DLT. Co-founders were David Sonstebo and Dominik Schiener.

IOTA Coordicide: Part of IOTA's plan for scalability with an outline at *coordicide.iota.org/*

IOTA Tangle DLT Main Net: IOTA transactions as shown at *tangle.glumb.de*.

IP: Internet Protocol, Intellectual Property.

IPC: Inter-Processor Communications as in DIF for RINA.

IRS: Internal Revenue Service.

ISP: Internet Service Provider.

JPM Coin: J. P. Morgan stablecoin.

KDP: Kindle Direct Publishing

Keccak-256: Hash used by Ethereum that uses Sponge construction.

KYC: Know Your Client, Know Your Customer.

LAN: Local Area Network.

law of networks: n(n-1)/2: Started with phone networks with n equal to the number of phones. With n = 1 phone, value is 0. With large n, value gets exponentially large with value near (n^2)/2.

LB: Lattice-Based.

LB-PKC: Lattice-Based Public Key Cryptography.

Libra: Facebook's plan for a new stablecoin and blockchain, that provides a platform for financial services innovation.

Lightning Network: A layer in the Bitcoin protocol that enables fast off-chain transactions between participating nodes.

MAC: Media Access Control. Used for physical device addresses. A MAC address is a number assigned by the manufacturer vs. an IP address that is a number assigned to a connection in a network.

message: Data in a crypto transaction that includes: from public address, to public address, and the amount.

mining: Method for verifying transactions for entry to a blockchain, and for settlement of transactions in a confirmed block, and to produce new crypto by solving a math problem.

mining fees: The payment to miners to verify transactions.

Miner-less: Method for transaction verification with an agent or client that does not require miners or their costs.

MIT: Massachusetts Institute of Technology.

Money: Defined in terms of three services: medium of exchange, store of value, unit of account; and six characteristics: durable, portable, divisible, uniform, limited supply, and acceptable.

MTL: Money Transmitter License.

NANO: Nano: A 5G pre-mined cryptocurrency with market values. Nano uses a DAG-based Block Lattice with double-entry Transaction ID (2xTXID) send and receive accounting. Founder was Colin LeMahieu.

national financial system: A Central Bank for a nation.

NE: North East.

non-peer wallets: Wallets that cannot be used for crypto transactions such as between Bitcoin and Ethereum wallets.

NSA: National Security Agency

OFDM: Orthogonal Frequency Division Multiplexing. A technique for wireless communications used in 4G and 5G and planned for 6G mobile wireless communications.

Off-Chain: Transactions are not recorded on a blockchain or DLT.

On-Chain: Transactions are recorded on a blockchain or DLT.

Owner of value in a wallet: Whoever has the private key.

passphrase: Password or phrase for account or wallet access.

PBOC: People's Bank of China.

peer-to-peer: Interchange between like things as in person-to-person, or Bitcoin wallet-to-Bitcoin wallet.

PKC: Public Key Cryptography. Method to sign a message with a private key but not reveal that private key, and to verify with a public key that a transaction has not been altered.

POS: Proof Of Stake. An alternative to POW to produce new cryptocurrencies.

POW: Proof Of Work. Computation performed by miners before new cryptocurrencies are produced.

pre-mined: A term used for crypto that is not mined and typically made available in the genesis block.

private key: A random character string used to compute a public key, digitally sign a message, and withdraw value from a wallet.

PSA: Payment Services Act (in Japan).

public address: A RIPEMD-160 and SHA-256 hash of a public key. To avoid visual errors, a Bitcoin address does not have number zero "0,"upper case o "O," lower case L "l," or upper case i "I."

public key: Computed from a private key using a variety of methods including ECDSA and Ed25519.

QR: Quick Response.

quantum computer: A computer with data represented as qubits, and theoretically superior to traditional computers with data represented as bits.

quantum security: Protocol design that makes it computationally unfeasible for a quantum computer to reveal a wallet's private key.

qubit: a quantum bit. Counterpart to a bit in classical computing. A qubit is the basic unit of information in a quantum computer.

Quorum: DLT for the JPM Coin.

Rehabilitation: Chapter 11: Debtor can reorganize its debts to try to re-emerge as a healthy entity.

RINA: Recursive Inter-Network Architecture. A common repeating function to for scalability. It was developed for mobile wireless communications and is used the Cardano ADA cryptocurrency.

RIPEMD-160: RACE Integrity Primitives Evaluation Message Digest-160. Hash of SHA-256 hashed public key to create a public address.

Ripple: Blockchain for the XRP pre-mined cryptocurrency.

RTGS: Real Time Gross Settlements. Method of fiat money transfer between banks. There is a separate RTGS for each sovereign nation, in contrast to a separate blockchain for each cryptocurrency.

Sat: Satoshi: Smallest unit of Bitcoin with 1 Sat = 0.00000001 BTC and 1 BTC = 100,000,000 Sat.

scalable: Designs that can increase capacity with increased transaction load. For example, a design that can increase from 10 transactions per second (tps) to 100 tps or 1,000 tps, as needed.

SEC: Securities and Exchange Commission.

seigniorage: Difference between face value and production cost of fiat money.

secp256k1: Elliptic curve parameters associated with Koblitz curve $y^2 = x^3 + 7$ used in Bitcoin and Ethereum.

settlement: An unconfirmed block of transactions becomes confirmed on a blockchain. To be compared with RTGS that provides fiat settlements between banks.

SHA-256: Secure Hash Algorithm-256. Cryptographic hash that generates a 256-bit text signature for a message of arbitrary length.

Sharding: A database partitioning technique to improve scalability.

signing algorithm: Use of public and private keys for secure message transmission over an insecure network.

soft fork: An agreed to change in a crypto protocol that does not result in a secondary blockchain or DLT.

sovereignty: Authority of a nation to shape its own destiny.

Sponge hash: A function that can take an input bit stream of any length and produce an output bit signature of any desired length.

stablecoin: Cryptocurrency with value pegged to fiat or other mechanism to remove volatility.

SSL: Secure Socket Layer: Encrypted link between server and browser.

sweep: Computer or smartphone optically scanning a private key to withdraw value stored in the associated wallet.

TBD: To Be Determined.

TDMA: Time Division Multiple Access. A method for mobile wireless communications, typically referred to as 2G.

Tether: See USDT.

TLS: Transport Layer Security. Naming of SSL after SSL 3.0.

ticker symbol: Sequence of characters representing traded assets.
token: Cryptocurrency based on ERC-20 Ethereum platform.
tps: transactions per second
transaction: Transfer of ownership of value.
Trinity Wallet: The IOTA wallet for smartphones and computers.
Troika: A cryptographic hash function for the use in IOTA and designed by CYBERCRYPT.

UK: The United Kingdom.
unconfirmed block: The newest block in a blockchain or DLT used for cleared but unconfirmed transactions.
UPS: United Parcel Service.
U.S.: United States.
USA: United States of America.
USD: United States Dollar.
USDC: USD Coin. A pre-mined cryptocurrency with stable value developed by Circle and Coinbase in the CENTRE consortium.
USDT: Tether. A pre-mined cryptocurrency with stable value issued by Tether Limited.
UTXO: Unspent Transaction Output. Can be spent as an input in a new transaction

wallet: A paired public address and private key with transactions recorded on a blockchain/DLT.
whale: Person or group with enough resources to affect the price of Bitcoin or Altcoin by buying or selling large quantities.
Wi-Fi: An Alliance of over 500 members, with wireless local area networking based on the IEEE 802.11 family of standards.
Winternitz: An algorithm that allows speed and storage tradeoffs to meet security objectives in digital signatures. Used by IOTA.
WIP: Work In Progress.
www: WWW: World Wide Web: Network-accessible information with links defined with http://www or secure https://www .

XRP: Pre-mined cryptocurrency with market value and transactions recorded on the Ripple blockchain. Founder was Chris Larsen.

Paper Wallets and QR Codes.

Wallets can be electronic or on paper. Bitcoin paper wallets can be created at *Bitaddress.org*. A wallet has a paired public address and private key with corresponding QR codes. The private key can be BIP0038 passphrase protected for more security. Paper wallets can be used for gifts, secure "cold" storage, and education on the crypto process by observing wallet transactions on the Blockchain ledger. Two examples show how QR codes are used with a Bitcoin app on a computer or smartphone.

The first example is a Bitcoin paper wallet with passphrase protection as shown in Figure 2.

Figure 2. Paper Wallet with Passphrase Protection

The public address is used for deposits via "send" to the QR code corresponding to: *1GX81UyD8EYwgZg3xFE3djLjiLAzMJSvka*. The QR code on the right is the passphrase protected private key corresponding to:

6PnNFmxkpxzLc6gHuw2NYLNfyfDhrpBAmcdUVWsdcnktoJSpNg7ztqzAae.

To withdraw value, **"sweep"** the private key with a Bitcoin app, then enter the passphrase (not shown but will be provided by the author to the first requesting non-family person). Deposit and withdraw transactions are recorded on the Blockchain at:

blockchain.com/btc/address/1GX81UyD8EYwgZg3xFE3djLjiLAzMJSvka

The second example is a Bitcoin paper wallet without passphrase protection as shown in Figure 3.

Figure 3. Paper Wallet without Passphrase Protection

To deposit value, "send" to the wallet's public address QR code corresponding to: *1BRFRuhnQTKg6M2bm1wk5vN1KUobqz4hFq*. The private key QR code for withdrawals on the right corresponds to:

L15fJvHwywpb4n5kssJr4BioA2ozmN4djsn2BZBV6pB28QafAgsJ

To withdraw value, sweep the private key with a Bitcoin app. Deposit and withdraw transactions are recorded on the Blockchain at:

blockchain.com/btc/address/1BRFRuhnQTKg6M2bm1wk5vN1KUobqz4hFq

For the prevention of double spends, if there were two or more copies of the wallet in Figure 3, the first copy used to withdraw value would leave an empty wallet as recorded on the Blockchain. If a second attempt was made to withdraw value, the wallet in Figure 3 would be empty and not recorded on the Blockchain.

Knowledge of how wallets work is key to understanding crypto and blockchains. Making deposits and withdrawals, and observing those transactions on a blockchain, could be the Wow factor that provides the motivation to learn more.

Epilogue

The Coiner Poem

Should I buy or should I sell
Every day, a new story to tell.
Bitcoin (BTC) or Ethereum (ETH) will likely win the day
Always with more crypto (currencies) in the fray.

A Satoshi (Sat) is a basic Bitcoin unit with 100 million Sat = 1 BTC
And when 1 Sat = $0.01 then 1 BTC = $1 million, golly gee.
A Blockchain is a distributed public ledger
That tracks wallet transactions and is very clever.

A wallet is a paired public address and private key
Like a mailbox address and owner's key, you see.
A wallet in a computer or smartphone is not tangible to hold
But is more like a bank that can store digital gold.

There are lots of hackers, since the Internet is not secure
But modern cryptography is there as a cure --
With a digital signature for every wallet transaction
Along with a public key to verify each signing action.

For those that crave stability, volatility is feared
Caused by day trading and people that are weird.
If you do play, security and 2FA are a priority
Otherwise you risk losing ownership authority.

Epilogue

For financial diversity, balance fiat for the future
With wallets in cold storage plus crypto on a computer.
Fiat has synergy with crypto -- the new money
But most have no idea or just think it's funny.

Fiat value is based on sovereign dictation
That debt justifies money creation.
In contrast, crypto value is based on math
With an elliptic curve providing a new path.

The Internet transfers packets without a central controller
Crypto transfers are similar without a 3rd party broker.
For those that are sad because they did not anticipate
Take time to learn more and "be ready" to participate.

Acknowledgement:
The Kipling Society, *The Coiner*, Circa 1611

John grew up in Pittston, a small town in NE Pennsylvania, with his four sisters. His favorite high school stories are about the Wilson Cloud Chamber science project and football legend "Jumpin" Johnny McHale. In college, John studied engineering and has degrees from Pennsylvania State University and Case Western Reserve University. After college, John worked as a systems engineer with AT&T and Motorola.

He is part of the American dream. His dad immigrated to the U.S. in the early 1900's. While his parents were only able to get elementary educations, John was able to get a graduate degree and contribute to the communications and now fintech industries.

John has two beautiful daughters and four wonderful grandchildren. What a difference a day makes. He held his first newborn grandson in the morning, and in the evening of the same day John had a first date with his wife to be Sherri.

After retirement, John teamed with his grandson on a dream to build a dune buggy powered with water. That dream included experimenting with electrolysis -- a method of converting water to HHO gas. After an explosive test with the HHO gas, that dream continues, but has been put on hold due to safety issues.

In his spare time, John now enjoys being an author, inventor, and website developer. Registered copyrights include those in this book and © 2018, TXu2125326, *Leveraging Time*. Patent US10204378B1 was granted in 2019 on *Flexible Payment Services*. His website and basis for this book is at *jmwnuk.wixsite.com/digitalassets*.

John and Sherri enjoy time with family and friends, and love to travel. The next destinations are always part of their fun travel planning.

Past

- Barter
- Evolution

Present

- Crypto Value
- Fiat Debt

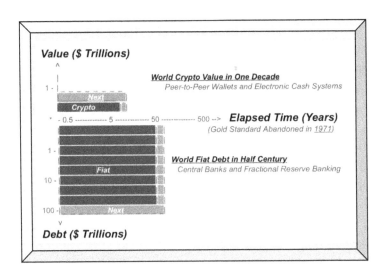

Future

- Verifiable
- Sustainable

www.ingramcontent.com/pod-product-compliance
Lightning Source LLC
Chambersburg PA
CBHW051215050326
40689CB00008B/1317